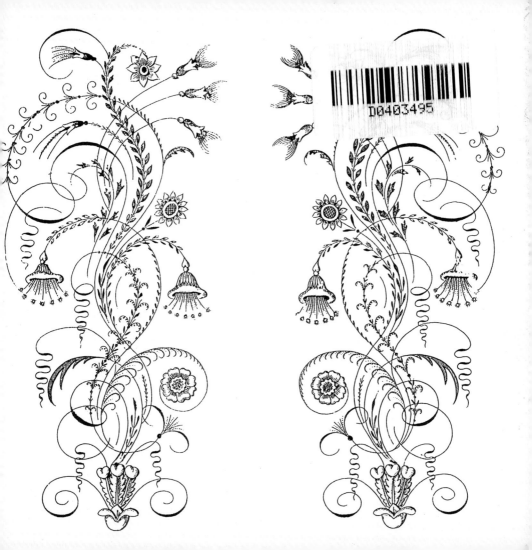

Carole Jean
from
Mom
Mother's Day May 9 1993

A Garden of Inspiration

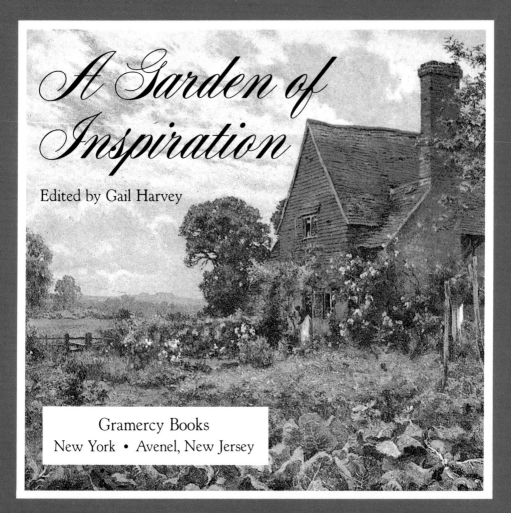

A Garden of Inspiration

Edited by Gail Harvey

Gramercy Books
New York • Avenel, New Jersey

Introduction and Compilation
Copyright © 1992 by Outlet Book Company, Inc.
First published in 1992 by Gramercy Books
distributed by Outlet Book Company, Inc.,
a Random House Company,
40 Engelhard Avenue
Avenel, New Jersey 07001

Manufactured in the United States

Designed by Liz Trovato

Library of Congress Cataloging-in-Publication Data
Garden of inspiration.
p.   cm.
ISBN 0-517-08141-5
1. Gardens—Literary collections.   2. Nature—Literary
collections.   3. Inspiration—Literary collections.
PN6071.G27G37   1992
808.8—dc20   92-10195   CIP

8 7 6 5 4 3 2 1

Introduction

"A moment's insight is sometimes worth a life's experience," wrote Oliver Wendell Holmes in the nineteenth century. This book is a provocative collection of the insights, in prose and poetry, of some of the world's most eminent writers and thinkers.

Ralph Waldo Emerson, for example, reflects on the way a woodland walk can salve his "worst wounds." Rabindranath Tagore considers the relationship of joy

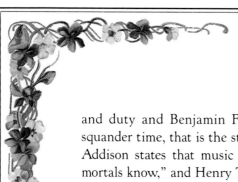

and duty and Benjamin Franklin writes "...do not squander time, that is the stuff life is made of." Joseph Addison states that music is "the greatest good that mortals know," and Henry Thoreau suggests that "We should be blessed if we lived in the present always, and took advantage of every accident that befell us."

Included, too, are moving poems by such great writers as Emily Dickinson, Robert Browning, James Russell Lowell, Alice Carey, and John Greenleaf Whittier.

This unusual book, illustrated with pastoral scenes painted by E.W. Waithe, will surely evoke pleasant memories, inspire hope and aspirations, and provide valuable insights for those who read and reread it.

GAIL HARVEY

New York
1992

*I*f I can stop one heart from breaking,
  I shall not live in vain;
If I can ease one life the aching,
  Or cool one pain,
Or help one lonely person
  Into happiness again
I shall not live in vain.

EMILY DICKINSON

The year's at the spring
And day's at the morn;
Morning's at seven;
The hillside's dew-pearled;
The lark's on the wing;
The snail's on the thorn;
God's in his heaven—
All's right with the world.

ROBERT BROWNING

*D*o all the good you can,
By all the means you can,
In all the ways you can,
In all the places you can,
At all the times you can,
To all the people you can,
As long as ever you can.

J<small>OHN</small> W<small>ESLEY</small>

If you have built castles in the air, your work need not be lost; that is where they should be. Now put foundations under them.

HENRY DAVID THOREAU

*D*o not fear going forward slowly;
fear only to stand still.

CHINESE PROVERB

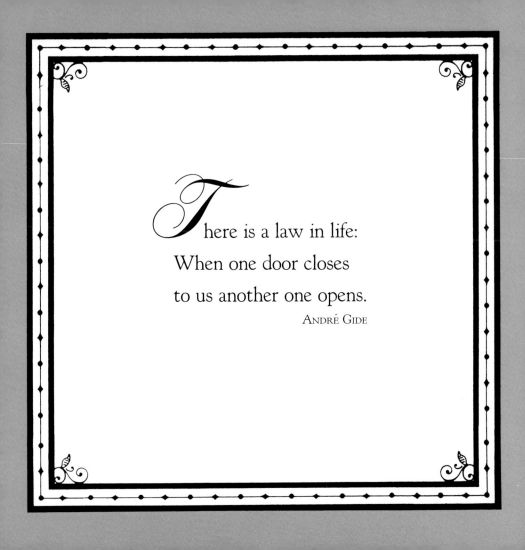

$\mathcal{T}$here is a law in life:
When one door closes
to us another one opens.

ANDRÉ GIDE

*A*ll my hurts
My garden spade can heal. A woodland walk,
A quest of river grapes, a mocking thrush,
A wild rose, a rock-loving columbine,
Salve my worst wounds.

RALPH WALDO EMERSON

I slept and dreamed
that life was joy,
I awoke and saw
that life was duty,
I acted and behold:
duty was joy.

RABINDRANATH TAGORE

The positive always defeats
the negative:
Courage overcomes fear;
Patience overcomes anger
and irritability;
Love overcomes hatred.

SWAMI SIVANANDA SARASVATI

The kiss of the sun for pardon,
  The song of the birds for mirth,
One is nearer God's Heart in a garden
  Than anywhere else on earth.

DOROTHY FRANCES GURNEY

$\mathcal{D}$on't commiserate with your fellow man. Help him.

MAXIM GORKY

*I*f any little word of mine
   May make some heart the lighter,
If any little song of mine
   May make some life the brighter,
God let me speak that little word
   And take my bit of singing
And plant it in some lonely vale
   To set the echoes ringing!

AUTHOR UNKNOWN

Oh! what is so rare as a day in June?
Then, if ever, come perfect days;
Then Heaven tries the earth if it be in tune,
And over it softly her warm ear lays:
Whether we look, or whether we listen,
We hear life murmur, or see it glisten.
Now the heart is so full that a drop overfills it,
We are happy now because God wills it.
No matter how barren the past may have been,
'Tis enough for us now that the leaves are green.

JAMES RUSSELL LOWELL

*N*ature ne'er deserts the wise and pure;
No plot so narrow, be but nature there,
No waste so vacant, but may well employ
Each faculty of sense and keep the heart
Awake to love and beauty.

SAMUEL TAYLOR COLERIDGE

*F*or the human heart is the mirror
Of the things that are near and far;
Like the wave that reflects in its bosom
The flower and the distant star.

ALICE CARY

*M*usic,

the greatest good

that mortals know,

And all of heaven

we have below.

JOSEPH ADDISON

$\mathcal{M}$usic alone
with sudden charms
can bind
The wand'ring sense,
and calm
the troubled mind.
WILLIAM CONGREVE

Field thoughts to me are happiness and joy,
Where I can lie upon the pleasant grass,
Or track some little path and so employ
My mind in trifles, pausing as I pass
The little wild flower clumps by, nothing nursed
But dews and sunshine and impartial rain;
And welcomely to quench my summer thirst
I bend me by the flaggy dyke to gain
Dewberries so delicious to the taste;
And then I wind the flag-fringed meadow lake
And mark the pike plunge with unusual haste
Through waterweeds and many a circle make,
While bursts of happiness from heaven fall;—
There all have hopes: here fields are free for all.

JOHN CLARE

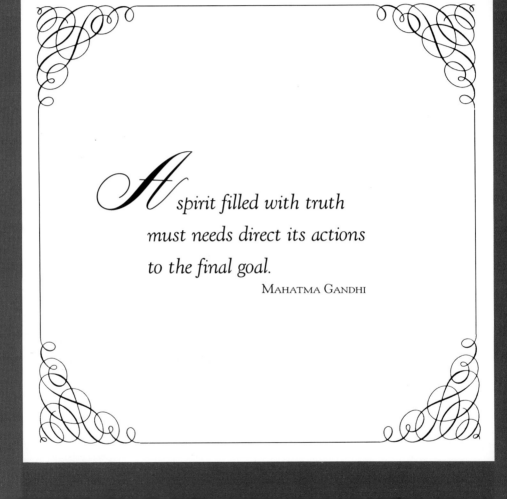

A spirit filled with truth
must needs direct its actions
to the final goal.

MAHATMA GANDHI

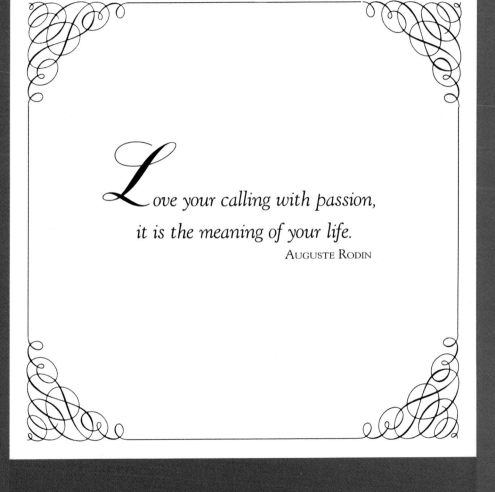

*L*ove your calling with passion,

it is the meaning of your life.

AUGUSTE RODIN

To be able to find joy in
another's joy: that is the
secret of happiness.

GEORGE BERNANOS

I am certain of nothing but the
holiness of the heart's affections
and the truth of the Imagination.
JOHN KEATS

In solitude
all great thoughts
are born.

MOSES HARVEY

*T*hose undeserved joys which come uncalled and make us more pleased than grateful are they that sing.

HENRY DAVID THOREAU

The best portion of a good man's life—
His little, nameless, unremembered acts
Of kindness and love.

WILLIAM WORDSWORTH

*I*t is the province
of knowledge to speak
and it is the privilege
of wisdom to listen.

OLIVER WENDELL HOLMES

*D*ost thou love life?
Then do not squander time,
for that is the stuff life
is made of.

BENJAMIN FRANKLIN

A single gentle rain makes the grass many shades greener. So our prospects brighten on the influx of better thoughts. We should be blessed if we lived in the present always, and took advantage of every accident that befell us, like the grass which confesses the influence of the slightest dew that falls on it; and did not spend our time in atoning for the neglect of past opportunities, which we call doing our duty. We loiter in winter while it is already spring.

HENRY DAVID THOREAU

There is no wealth
but life.

JOHN RUSKIN

Summer is prodigal of joy. The grass
Swarms with delighted insects as I pass,
And crowds of grasshoppers at every stride
Jump out all ways with happiness their guide;
And from my brushing feet moths flirt away
In safer places to pursue their play.
In crowds they start. I marvel, well I may,
To see such worlds of insects in the way,
And more to see each thing, however small,
Sharing joy's bounty that belongs to all.
And here I gather, by the world forgot,
Harvests of comfort from their happy mood,
Feeling God's blessing dwells in every spot
And nothing lives but owes him gratitude.

JOHN CLARE

Beauty in things exists in the mind which contemplates them.

DAVID HUME

A moment's insight

is sometimes worth

a life's experience.

<small>OLIVER WENDELL HOLMES</small>

Speak nought, move not, but listen, the sky is full of
    gold.
No ripple on the river, no stir in field or fold,
All gleams but nought doth glisten, but the far-off
    unseen sea.

Forget days past, heart broken, put all memory by!
No grief on the green hillside, no pity in the sky,
Joy that may not be spoken fills mead and flower and
    tree.

WILLIAM MORRIS

The holiest of all holidays are those

Kept by ourselves in silence and apart;

The secret anniversaries of the heart.

HENRY WADSWORTH LONGFELLOW

To see a world in a grain of sand
And a heaven in a wild flower,
Hold infinity in the palm of your hand
And eternity in an hour.

WILLIAM BLAKE

The autumn time has come;
On woods that dream of bloom,
And over purpling vines,
The low sun fainter shines.

The aster flower is failing,
The hazel's gold is paling;
Yet overhead more near
The eternal stars appear.

And present gratitude
Insures the future's good,
And for the things I see
I trust the things to be;

That in the paths untrod,
And the long days of God,
My feet shall still be led,
My heart be comforted.

JOHN GREENLEAF WHITTIER

$\mathcal{F}$aith is the subtle chain
which binds us to the
infinite.

ELIZABETH OAKES SMITH

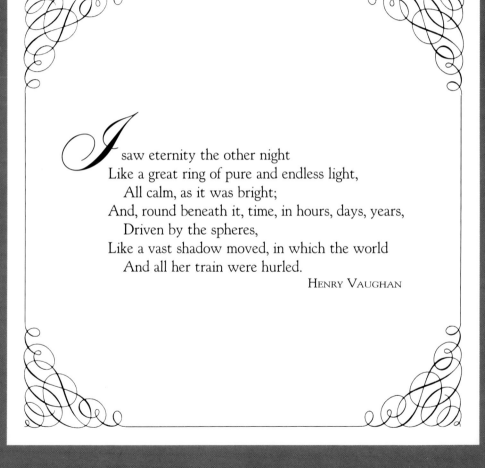

I saw eternity the other night
Like a great ring of pure and endless light,
    All calm, as it was bright;
And, round beneath it, time, in hours, days, years,
    Driven by the spheres,
Like a vast shadow moved, in which the world
    And all her train were hurled.

HENRY VAUGHAN

$\mathcal{M}$en grind and grind in the mill of a truism, and nothing comes out but what was put in. But the moment they desert the tradition for a spontaneous thought, then poetry, wit, hope, virtue, learning, anecdote, all flock to their aid.

RALPH WALDO EMERSON

Tell me not, in mournful numbers,
  "Life is but an empty dream!"
For the soul is dead that slumbers,
  And things are not what they seem.
      HENRY WADSWORTH LONGFELLOW

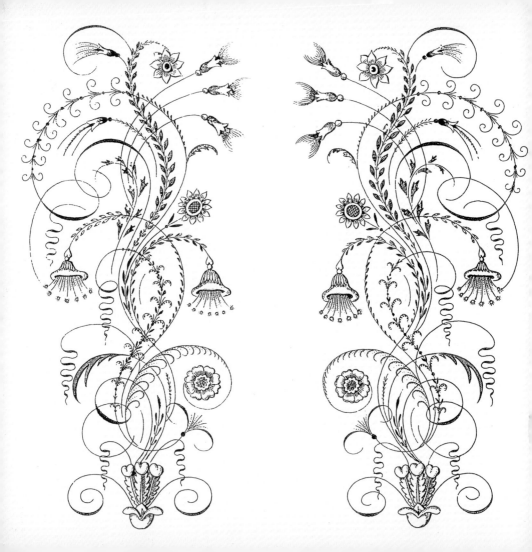